Locked in Different Alphabets

Poetry is the key
to the hieroglyphics of nature

~ David Hare

Also by Doris Fiszer

Sasanka (Wild Flower), Bywords Publications, 2018
The Binders, Tree Press, The Tree Reading Series, 2016

Locked in Different Alphabets

by
Doris Fiszer

720 Sixth Street, Unit #5
New Westminster, BC
V3L 3C5
CANADA

Title: Locked in Different Alphabets
Author: Doris Fiszer
Publisher: Silver Bow Publishing
Cover Layout/Design: Candice James
Editing: Candice James

All rights reserved including the right to reproduce or translate this book or any portions thereof, in any form without the permission of the publisher. Except for the use of short passages for review purposes, no part of this book may be reproduced, in part or in whole, or transmitted in any form or by any means, either by means electronically or mechanically, including photocopying, recording, or any information or storage retrieval system without prior permission in writing from the publisher or a licence from the Canadian Copyright Collective Agency (Access Copyright).

www.silverbowpublishing.com
info@silverbowpublishing.com
ISBN: 978-1-77403-106-3 paperback
ISBN: 978-1-77403-107-0 electronic book
© Silver Bow Publishing

Library and Archives Canada Cataloguing in Publication

Title: Locked in different alphabets / by Doris Fiszer.
Names: Fiszer, Doris, 1953- author.
Description: Poems.
Identifiers: Canadiana (print) 20200254278 | Canadiana (ebook) 20200254316 | ISBN 9781774031063
   (softcover) | ISBN 9781774031070 (ebook)
Classification: LCC PS8611.I8275 L63 2020 | DDC C811/.6—dc23

Locked in Different Alphabets

For my family

Barbara (Wolska) Fiszer (1929-1999)

Andrew Fiszer (1924-2014)

and George Fiszer (1950-2009)

Locked in Different Alphabets

Testimonials

Family is something all humans share but every family is different. In these touching poems, Doris Fiszer explores her own family, her parents, her brother. She touches on and delves into their frailties, their strengths, all the myriad moments and characteristics that made them unique. From the Nazi camps of World War II in Poland to the suburbs of Ottawa, Fiszer reveals how family is like a garden: it grows, it survives, it fades and dies. She reveals how we are all locked in a garden of different alphabets. ~ Mark Frutkin, author of "Fabrizio's Return"; "Atmosphere Apollinaire"; "Hermit Thrush" and "The Rising Tide".

***

With gentleness and exquisite control, Doris Fiszer explores the legacy of a family displaced by war, following its origins from the Nazi war camps to the next generation's lives in Canada. This is a moving and tender tribute to survival and the mysterious ways that each life must end and how people who love must let go. In the face of the trauma of the past, here also is beauty and an ability to receive the mysterious solace of kinship and nature. ~ Nadine McInnis, author of "Blood Secrets" and "Delirium for Solo Harp"

***

These tough yet tender poems are replete with deft images of grief, frustration, humour and deep love, like stiffly beaten egg whites stirred into the batter of family life, folding light and air into serious themes. Their honesty speaks of who we are, and the courage demanded of love. ~ Claudia Coutu Radmore, author of "Your Hands Discover Me" and "Accidentals".

***

Doris Fiszer's Locked In Different Alphabets is a moving portrait of a Polish immigrant family living with the traumatic legacy of the Nazi concentration camps of the Second World War. In these rich and unsettling lyric poems Fiszer confronts her subject head-on, with unwavering compassion and grace. ~ Deanna Young Poet Laureate of Ottawa, Ontario and author of "Reunion" and "House of Dreams".

***

Table of Contents

My Brother George ... 13

George in Grade 1... 15
Altar Boys ... 16
Nightly Frights ... 17
Trapped ... 18
Voiceless ... 19
Testing ... 20
George's Shadow Puppets ... 21
Hurt You More ... 22
My Parents' Getaway ... 24
Pyrolysis ... 25
Treading Water ... 26
Forewarned ... 27
Voiceless 2 ... 28
No Returns ... 30
Months ... 31
So Long ... 32
Turn of a Phrase ... 33
What My Departed Do ... 34
Family Visit ... 35

My Father Andrzej ... 37

My Father Tells Me About His Childhood ... 39
Snapshot 1 ... 41
Our Single ... 42
Shawl ... 43
Still ...44
Another Winter Has Taken More of You ... 45
I've Never Asked ... 46
Binders ... 47
Retreat ... 49
Nursing Home Garden ... 50

Useful ... 51
No Time for Visitors ... 52
Psychiatrist ... 53
His Story in Bits and Pieces ... 54
Phone Call ... 55
Inalienable Rights ... 56
Snapshot 2 ... 57
Stepping Off on the Fifth Floor ... 58
In Context ... 59
Semi-Annual Nursing Home Evaluation Meeting ... 60
A Deep Breath ... 61
Sunday Sermon at the Long-Term Facility ... 62
Origins ... 63
Voice Mail from My Father ... 64
Cardinal ... 65
My Fault ... 66
A Reasonable Request ... 67
Rattling Down the Chimney ... 68
Two Things ... 69
Tool Chests ... 70
Disappearing ... 71
Future Gardens ... 73
No One Can ...74
Exhale ... 75
Auction ... 76
Counter-Clockwise ... 77
I Never Had the Chance ... 78
Lately, Everything is Language ... 79

My Mother, Sasanka, Means Wild Flower ... 81

Ashes ... 83
My Parents Remember ... 84
Babcia (Grandmother) ... 85
I Knew ... 86
Sasanka (Wild Flower) ... 87

Słoneczko ... 89
Without Warning ... 90
My Mother Said ... 91
Bell's Corners ... 92
Labour ... 93
Dreams Over and Over ... 94
In Each Other's Dreams ... 95
Salt Spray ... 96
Understanding My Mother's Worries ... 97
Passenger ... 98
Foraging ... 99
Snapshot 3 ... 100
Zen Garden ... 101

Acknowledgements ... 102

Locked in Different Alphabets

Locked in Different Alphabets

My Brother George

Locked in Different Alphabets

George in Grade 1

Mother's hands
tremble
after she hangs up the phone.

She slips a cardigan over my dress,
the one with the embroidered ladybug
on the collar, unable to fasten the buttons.

She grabs
her purse and cigarettes, pulls
me by the hand all the way there.

As soon as we get to the school a nun
in black habit, white wimple, veil
and crucifix

waddle-walks up like a gigantic penguin
towards us, shoving my brother
in front of her.

He started a fire in the boys' bathroom.
Don't bring him back
until he behaves.

At home my father's ear-splitting thunder
and the haze of their cigarette smoke
thickening the air.

Altar Boys

Angelic in his black cassock,
and starched-white surplice, George

lights six high candles on the main altar.
(My brother loves playing with fire).

He and Janusz, take turns
responding to the priest in Latin.

George presents the bowl and pitcher,
pours water over the priest's hands.

Janusz unfolds a fresh towel, holds
it while Father Twardowski dries his fingers.

George swings the incense burner elatedly.
Sweet-scented smoke puffs out in clouds.

The boys bow in unison each time
the priest holds up bread and wine.

George shakes the altar bells, a coveted duty.
Janusz leans over and snatches them.

A blaze of blasphemies and the brawl is on—
bare knuckles at the altar.

In his defense George said
but it was my turn to ring the bells!

Locked in Different Alphabets

Nightly Frights

My big brother and I fling
his plushy Rin-Tin-Tin

back and forth
from his bed to mine

it smacks the wall a few times,
crashes to the floor,

a snowstorm of fluff
in the dark.

Mother puts me to bed
in Babcia's room until I'm asleep

carries me back to my bed again,
convinced George is sleeping.

He whispers *a monster is under the bed*,
    pretends to strangle me.

I wake up screaming.
George doesn't say sorry

until Father comes in,
    starts unbuckling his belt.

Mother lies down beside me,
    pats my hair.

A ghostly hand hovers
over my head again tonight as I try to sleep.

Trapped

The radio is always turned off
so my dad can focus as he steers with one hand
and flaps the other at us to be quiet.

The windows are closed and both my parents
are smoking. *George, stop hurting your sister*
my mother says.

My father pulls to the shoulder
telling George to get out, then slowly drives
beside him while he walks. I wave to him.

Modeling my father,
our Nash Rambler spits out
the usual ill-tempered rattles.

My brother gets back in
gets sick on the seat
and on me

and I am trapped, trapped in the smell
I will always associate
with that day.

In front of the giraffes' enclosure
Father photographs us. A giraffe bends its neck,
snatches my mother's wide-brim hat.

Voiceless

This morning
my brother,
                after Father warned
                you better be nice
                to your sister today,

sits beside me on the glider swing,
helps brush my doll's nylon hair,
ties a ribbon around her ponytail
and washes her face with a damp cloth.

From green velvet scraps
in our mother's sewing basket
he is trying to sew a new dress
for Chatty Cathy.

I thread the needle for him.

Yesterday,
he punched my Chatty Cathy in the stomach
swung her by her curls over his head like a lasso,
hurled her into the mud breaking her voice box.

Testing

We collect grass and wild flowers
for the caterpillars, spiders and toads
I gather in jars, he hammers
holes in their lids.

Before bed, George dares me
not to hold my nose
in the outhouse, dares me
to look into its pit;

bangs
the door shut,
locking me in there,

won't   let   me   out…

Locked in Different Alphabets

George's Shadow Puppets

his hands and voice conjure
                       a carnival
                                  of comic book characters

                    eagle flies
     higher and higher in the sky,
                          cottontail clasped in its claws

                    baby elephant tap-dances,
                          chants the alphabet song

                  two   moose
                        lock antlers
                                wrestle each other
                                    to the ground

                  crocodile
o   p   e   n   s   w   i   d   e
                  shows its teeth

                    our   laughter
        ping   pongs
                  into

                semi-
                darkness

Hurt You More

George corners me in our
   gloomy hallway   locks
       my arms in a throbbing grip.
If you tell, I'll hurt you more.

Father slips in silently,
       closes my bedroom door.
Keep an eye on George
       he hisses, wags his finger in my face.
On my way to gym class—
       my big brother in the grade 13 lounge
      dealing cards to the usual trio.

For once let's have a peaceful dinner
       Mother tells Father.
He nose-dives into his usual sermon—
       if only George weren't so lazy.
He won't amount to anything
       without an education.

Change the topic Mother says.
Were you in class today?
       he asks George.

Did you see him playing poker
       with the three other flunkies?

If you love him you'll tell me Father says to me.

George races towards his bedroom,
       Father on his tail
    I disappear
   clutching car keys, slam the door.

Locked in Different Alphabets

I ride the escalator
              up   and
                        down
              the three levels of Bayshore mall.

Mother warms my dinner.
                He's finally studying.
On my way to bed,
        I see George, at his desk,
bowed over his math text.
        a *MAD* magazine's cover
                  exposed   in its pages.
He shuts the book when he sees me—

Another wakeful night

       my bed—
          a

t
     o
        s
           s
               i
                   n
                      g
s
    h
      i
        p

       in the whirlwind.

My Parents' Getaway

Stop I yell. *Get off!*
When I struggle to push my brother away
he pins both arms
behind my back with one hand

and keeps on tickling me
on the kitchen floor.
His newly-adult body—
a rock that flattens
my breath and purples my skin.

Mother has an intuition.
Something's not right at home she tells my father.
Turn   the   car   around.
Father grabs George, whacks him
with his leather belt

again and again.
That's enough.
Mother and I shout.
I still have dreams about it.

I feel as though I'm cornered
in a pitch-dark cave.
A shadowy form presses,
presses against me.

Pyrolysis

After the time George set
the kitchen curtains ablaze
I was afraid to be
alone with him.

He'd washed the ashes
down the drain, waved away
layers of grey haze
that choked us both.

My hands still shake
when I strike a match.
A whiff of smoke
can sharpen my breath

hasten my step
make me think …
        escape.

Treading Water

It started in the lake—
my brother's elbows and hands held out of the water.
Strengthens the legs and lungs George said,
skills acquired from his life guard summers.

You were the golden girl.
The word golden hung
over the lake—

a veil   between us.
I hated you most of the time.
Mother loved you more.

The past bubbled up from the lake's depths.

Being golden had its price I said.
Nothing I do is good enough
for Father. Even my degree is the wrong one.
We swam closer to the truth that afternoon.

It started in the lake—
the lake listening to us laugh
lightheartedly as children

the lake witnessing our bobbing bodies
drawing closer, watching us float
into gentler water.

Though my brother offered me his hand,
helped me onto the dock and handed me a towel,
everything familiar looked broken,
the ground beneath me   shaking.

Forewarned

George,
      flaunting new swim trunks,
      an early June glow, well-toned thighs,
      and playfully flexed biceps,
springs into the deep.

Twenty flawless lengths,
water-weight routine, chin-ups
off the diving board's edge.

A toast of champagne
to his health, a raucous burst of *Sto Lat,*
the Polish birthday song:
niech zyje nam
may   you   live   to   be   a   hundred.

Grilled lamb,
lemon-roasted potatoes,
honey-soaked baklava,
blueberry-filled pierogi,
free-flowing Sangria.

Summer barbeque
with unpredicted
storm   clouds.

Voiceless 2

I used to be so active George said
when he could still speak.
One blink. Yes

to a strong rum and coke.
He can still suck and swallow.
Two blinks. No

to pasta and puréed meatballs.
Afraid of choking. Two blinks. No
to a feeding tube

when he could still sign his name
on the living will.
Slurred trickle of words

soon cease.
His body—
a flash-frozen pond.

Biking legs and feet—
are stones on the wheelchair's footstool.
Fingers no longer hover

over the spelling board
for the precise letter.
Hands warped into ice-grey hooks.

I uncurl each finger,
rub heat into my brother's hands,
massage rigid shoulders.

We hold up each CD
from his vast collection,
One blink. Yes

to Elton John,
Elvis's "Christmas Album",
Led Zeppelin's "Stairway to Heaven".

One blink. Yes
to another drink.

Dad teases George it's the perfect time
to strum his guitar,
good exercise for his fingers.

My husband winks at George
and he winks back,
grunts as though to laugh.

One blink. Yes
to another log in the fireplace

we keep the fire   raging
the way he likes it.

No Returns

After Mother's unexpected death
when George was still well

George and Father had haunted
the Stittsville flea market, haggled

over porcelain, clocks, lamps,
they loaded the trunk and back seat

collecting throw-aways on garbage days,
Saturdays, retail therapy at the mall—

mounds of marked-down socks and plaid shirts
choked drawers and closets.

Over a lunch of Father's turkey soup,
rye bread, Polish pickles, herring,

Zywiec beer, they scoured newspaper ads
for open houses,

circled upcoming garage sales, fantasized life
on a farm in Quebec, in a condo on Clearwater Beach

unveiled their dreams to George's wife
when real estate agents called.

Months

I lost my best buddy my father said when George died.

only five months
for ALS to shrivel
his son's muscles to fibre

Father swiftly shifted
from steadying missteps with a walking stick
averting tumbles with a walker—
to staring
at four blank walls
in a wheelchair

So Long

The day after George died
I watched a chickadee pluck red berries
from the snow-laden bush
outside my kitchen window.

A van pulled out of the laneway
across the street—

the license plate read
SEW LONG.

For weeks, our living room light bulbs
buzzed like trapped bees in a jar,
flashed on and off
in the dark.

Turn of a Phrase

The dead keep coming back—
in the turn of a phrase,
a stranger's walk,
the certain way a head bends.

My mother
still makes tea,
sets the table for two,
tells me I'm too thin.

On the phone Father still asks
the same question again and again.
Is Mother with you?
Don't tire her. I miss her.

I turn to look at my mother
but she's gone.

My brother stands beside a lake,
granite hills behind him.
Look at me. I can still walk and talk
then cycles off.

What My Departed Do

my dead linger
    in every crevice of this room
  make unwound clocks toll
     in unsynchronized hours
  on the rosewood-framed mirror
    flicks of their breath

they leave mutterings behind doors
    shift and change places in the air
      murmur and sigh

in the nook by the stairs
    a desk brimming with apple-scented candle
      a Swiss Army Knife rusty blades

  they make sure I notice compasses
     and whistles
       from mushroom-picking days

outside the window
    a half-moon
  is misted   by December's shadow
    night's snow-dust
      heaps against a wall
    dark soon yields to pale sun

      and my departed ones
       are responsible for it all

Family Visit

I lean into the shifting temperature
of the graveyard,
follow the pebbled pathway
past manicured plots, marble monuments
to row number 27.

They all greet me at once:
familiar voices, high-pitched,
soft or gravelly.

I rest a red rose
on the family stone
offer a prayer,
tidy their gravesite,

watch a milk-white butterfly
swirl like an aspen leaf.

Locked in Different Alphabets

Locked in Different Alphabets

My Father Andrzej

Locked in Different Alphabets

My Father Tells Me About His Childhood

My father was a doctor, an addict, womanizer
but also a caregiver and friend to everyone
except those who needed him most.

Be strong for your mother, sister and brother
my grandparents told me.
When Father reappeared after months of absence

my mother swept his sins
into a dustpan, aired out
the sour scents of other women.

My sister fluttered around him,
a tender leaf in the breeze.

I carried my home on my shoulders
when Father drifted,
minded Magda and Wojtek,
peeled potatoes, scraped carrots for veal stew.

I won't let him stay
Mother said again.

Your father, such a disappointment
my grandparents said.

I planted sunflowers in their vegetable garden
found haven
in their home and in the tree house,
a weeping birch in their yard.

I asked God to help me forgive,
prayed for strength not to kill him.

*At nineteen
I was arrested
for political reasons*

*sent to Gross Rosen Concentration Camp Germany
escaped found myself on a train going back to Krakow*

*I don't remember how I escaped
or got on that train*

*the German guard who arrested me the first time
saw me and sent me back*

I didn't try to escape again

trapped bird
another attempt
to take wing

Snapshot 1

On Sundays
our home breathes quietly,
doesn't rumble with his rage,
or bristle with the usual workday hurry.

My father whistles "This Old Man"
in the kitchen. Bacon crackles.

I sing *this old man he played one*
he played knick-knack on my thumb.

Steaming cocoa. Soft clouds.
Scrambled eggs. Buttered rye toast.
Plum jam.

Father smiles. Lifts a finger,
Mother's sleeping.

Our Single

You blamed everything on me—
that new doctor you recommended

A time bomb ticked
behind the gloss of your charm
and repertoire of jokes,
your laughter tumbling
into brooding silence.

You disapproved
of my boyfriends, enforced curfews,
had me followed after I moved out,
blamed me
your mother would still be alive if...

We didn't speak for months,
sometimes for years.

Still, once long ago
we cut a single together
of a Polish love song,
you held my hand while we sang,
your deep baritone in harmony
with my four-year old soprano—
you patted my head when we finished.

Shawl

You were watching as she slept
and while you whispered her name
she disappeared.

The sixty pounds you tried to lose
when she was alive
slipped off your bones.

You couldn't stop listening
to the incessant chatter of your radios,
each one tuned to a different station.

When you stayed up late
her voice still directed
you to go to bed.

Sorting her clothes, you presented me
with her cherished black shawl threaded with silver.
I lost the love of my life.

I saw you cry for the first time, sensed
the brokenness in your step.

Still

I don't recognize this man
whose steps shuffle
as if his body were a burden.

I don't recognize
the shrunken belly;
his voice, once booming,
now whispers in raspy monotones.

Age unravels him,
exposes the rawness
dampening the flash
in his green eyes,
rattling his scientific mind
though he would deny it.

He still plays bridge,
swims laps in his condo pool,
monitors his blood sugar.

Yet he seems eager to move on
though he won't discuss it
since he doesn't know
where he's going or when.

Another Winter Has Taken More of You

The walker you use, railing you had installed
to navigate four stairs from the dining area
to the living room, not so bad
when you still remember everything.

We listen to your antique clocks—
synchronized chimes mark the hour.

In the living room, we view
the river through your window.

Last night I dreamt you walked away,
an overpacked suitcase in one hand,
waving good-bye with the other ...

before a snow squall buried all signs of you.

I've Never Asked

I'm having trouble doing something

    What is it you can't do?

I freeze I can't walk I can't open the fridge
I forgot what the can opener is for and
when I remembered I opened the wrong can

    Have you eaten today?

I can't remember if I have or when —
what time is it

    It's after four.
    You need to eat dinner soon.

I've never asked for your help —
I need it now

Locked in Different Alphabets

Binders

We study your collection of sixty or more binders
brimming with documents
each one enshrined in a plastic sleeve.

You explain certificates and government papers,
the years spent in Nazi camps,
wedding photos of you and Mother,
post-war Germany,
the voyage to Canada on the *General J.H. McRae.*

You show me certificates and diplomas
from your working days at Nortel.

> *I'll bring most of these binders to the nursing home*

You wind your seven antique clocks.

> *I'll need a few of my clocks*

You linger over your collection of hand-painted china.

> *I want some of my porcelain too*

You describe a precision instrument
from lab work at Nortel—
a complicated-looking device
that measures the width of a strand of hair.

> *do you want it*

> I'll take some of the clocks
> Mother's paintings
> photo albums.

I've changed my mind I'm not going
I can't live in one room

We hang photos, antique clocks,
hide tool boxes under the bed and in the closet,
squeeze things into the dresser and night table.

I'll need my teak book case for my binders

I cut up your hamburger
help you in and out of your chair.

Retreat

When I enter his room
a swarm of words prick.
I unleash my grudges
with equal fury.

Fighting leads to more fighting—
despite everything, he's my father, an ailing man
and I love him.

I leave him sputtering in his wheelchair.

In the elevator I count breaths
almost succeed in slowing my racing heart,
wave to the receptionist in the lobby
as though everything were fine.

Before I see him again
I imagine an artist
painted over our last encounter,
stippled softer tones
onto a fresh canvas.

Nursing Home Garden

I help put on your hat and clip-on sunglasses
I fill your vest's seven pockets
with gum, mint candies,
Bailey's chocolates, three faded handkerchiefs,
pack the small basket attached to your wheelchair
with tapes of Polish love songs, extra batteries,
bottles of water, a box of Kleenex.

You balance the radio on your lap.
I maneuver you past the black-eyed Susans.

> *stop there look at those figurines*
> *turn right keep going get closer*
> *I want a better look at those flowers*

We gaze at the pink clematis.

> *I need some small containers to collect seeds*
> *from flowers like those over there I need my clay pots*
> *shovel and earth from my condo storage locker*

You sing along to love songs.

> *I'm on the garden committee I've tried everything*
> *since I've been here exercise class*
> *resident committee choir*
> *I'm still trying to get bridge going*
> *let's go back*

I offer a spoonful of vegetable broth.

Useful

the guard asked us
if anyone was a barber
I said I was
when I had to shave
a man's pubic hair
I froze
the guard asked me
why I said I was a barber
when I wasn't
so I wouldn't be killed
made myself become his friend

fresh blood on
razored
skin

No Time for Visitors

He shuffles and reshuffles documents
from one binder to another,
spreads papers on the floor, bed, chair
asks my help to reorder them,
replaces folders precisely on shelves,
rearranges his room again.

move that lamp under the window
take that small table beside the door
move it beside my bed
push the fan closer to the wall
hide the cord under the base
no I don't like my room that way
move everything back the way it was

I push his wheelchair close to the phone,
dial her number,
hand him the receiver.

she's resting

He reaches for his Nortel binder,
leafs through safety magazines,
doesn't look up
when I say good-bye.

Psychiatrist

I spent two hours with your dad today.
The whole time he showed me what's in his binders,
obsessed about relabeling and reorganizing them.
I had to leave the room to refocus.
I've started him on medication.

Good.
Yesterday he wanted to die.

His Story in Bits and Pieces

*I assembled V-1 and V-2 rockets
that were used to bomb London
American space technology comes from Dora
there were over 60,000 prisoners mostly Poles
in the underground concentration camp*

*I survived because I was sick
lost hearing in my left ear
after I got better
two doctors asked me
to help out in the hospital
I was one of the lucky ones*

*One of the attendants
who helps me get dressed in the mornings
knows someone who survived Dora
wants to bring us together*

I'm still living that trauma

our deaf world
repeating what
it doesn't want to hear

Phone Call

you signed for the wheelchair

it's your fault it's too small

I called the guy yesterday

he never showed up call him now

I need my granddaughter's phone number

last time you wrote the numbers down I couldn't read them

slow down I can't hear you speak into the phone

This time my husband answers my father's call.
What did my dad say? I ask.

He said *you can take your numbers*
and shove them you know where.

I play Schubert's "Serenade" on the piano,
over and over.

I can still hear his accusations.

Inalienable Rights

call the German Embassy again he demands
they need to know I'm in a wheelchair

He is proud of always being unreasonable
and loud in his insistence
that he is never going to change.

Exercising later on the gym's elliptical machine
I chant my mantra:

        I   will
                        live   through   this.

My resentments towards my father—
      streams of sweat.

Snapshot 2

In shallow water
we swallow the light,
climb lattices of milky foam,
laughter flashes like silver,
a wave-rush presses us close.

I rest in the curve of my father's shoulder.
Salt scents the crevices of his skin.

Our outlines sculpted
in the sandy shore

water-washed by next tide.

Stepping Off on the Fifth Floor

Ellen and Lorna again (whom I've met before)
are in their wheelchairs in front of the elevator,
emaciated Ellen in a flowered suit with lace collar,
clutches my hand, doesn't let go.

Crimson nails stab my skin.
You were always such a good girl she says.

Lorna, fleshy in stained orange dress, asks,
if I can push her to the dining room.
She cries. I stroke her damp head,
fasten her bib, push her closer to the table.

I picture my father
flapping around his room—
cawing like an angry crow.

> *Where are you?*
> *Why are you late?*

I picture myself
alone one day
like Ellen and Lorna.

I let him wait.

In Context

you think when someone doesn't talk to you
at school that's a problem
I saw people hung from trees
dead bodies lying on the street
people kill themselves after we were liberated
because they didn't have anyone to go home to
come back when you have something real to complain about

clouds
outside your window
stifle the sun

Semi-Annual Nursing Home Evaluation Meeting

I flattened your hair
with a wet brush this morning
but it still bristles like a porcupine's quills
… like you.

My father's loud
>who called the meeting
>move me closer
>my wheelchair's not right
>why can't I have an electric one

>that coloured nurse
>all she ever did was sit in her kitchen
>before she came here

The doctor checks his watch.

>the fat one yells at me to move faster
>knows I'm in a wheelchair

The doctor gets up to leave
barely conceals a smile.

You are red-faced
and your hair still bristles.

>was I too rough

   Yes.

>good they'll try harder next time

A Deep Breath

Today the white light I conjure in my mind
to protect me from your outbursts,
sucks up your black mood like a sponge.

I unlock the bolted box
holding the rage
that scorches your room red.

You follow me home,
sit on my shoulder all evening,
slip into my night, in a dream
you and I are crammed into the back seat
of our 1959 Nash Rambler,
pointing fingers at each other, shouting.

When I wake
I listen to the rain,
watch a cardinal
resting on the mock orange tree
and prepare myself
to visit you again.

Sunday Sermon at the Long-Term Care Facility

"Is anyone awake?" the white-haired priest asks.
"Just checking.
Who has looked after a sick husband or wife?
All of you, I bet. If I weren't celibate,
I might have married a wonderful woman
or a nasty one. You never know.
I could have been divorced
a few times by now."

The priest tells us a joke
about a minister, rabbi and priest
who try to get rid of bats
from their churches.

My father, my husband and I laugh.
The man beside me wakes,
drops the hymn book. An attendant picks it up,
opens it to the hymn we are going to sing
but he is asleep again
holding the book upside down.

Over lunch I tell my father
I don't remember mass being so entertaining
when I was growing up.

He whispers
I had to gently tug on your ear
to get you to sit still at church
you were only happy
when you sang along with the choir

Origins

after the war on my way
to a liberation camp in Germany
I helped a woman and girl
put their bags on the train
I found out they were mother and daughter
the woman pretended she knew me
told the official I was her nephew
since he thought we were related
he let us travel together
and live as family in the camp
that was your mother and her mother
that's when I fell in love with your mother

some plants
flourish
after winter

Voice Mail from My Father

I'm at the Polish Embassy
it's being bombed

EMERGENCY EMERGENCY EMERGENCY

get me out
they're trying to kill me
pick up the phone I know you're there

Cardinal

I pull back your curtains
open your window
clear out winter's ghost.

The cardinal sings high on a pine nearby.
Just shadows you say when I point out the bird.

On the sill a pot of daisies we forgot to water
leaves turned sickly green,
gnarled roots exposed,
watering our last ritual.
I help steady your stubborn hands.

You mumble *I love you.*
I can hardly hear you,
a prelude to your grand finale,
confession,
remorse coughed up
like a sputtering engine
smoothing edges,
gaining momentum,
then petering out.

My Fault

I clean chocolate drippings from your chin,
reposition your wheelchair and hold your cup
so you can sip ginger ale
and smooth your unruly hair with a damp brush.

It's hard to understand your shaky whispers
but it's clearly my fault
you're in the wrong wheelchair.

You have always pointed out my flaws
rather than praising me
the list of all the things I do wrong
rings in my head.

Yet, I'm told that you always ask others
did you meet my daughter
that's her picture on the wall

An extra bowl of chocolate gelato
for dessert.
His proud words fill my mouth
with added sweetness.

A Reasonable Request

I've been on the waiting list for over nine months
for that room on the fourth floor
it's double the size of mine
Gladys who lives there is sick
I don't wish her any harm but I want that room
my rosewood bookcase would fit perfectly
under her window
I want to see the room again
let's go ask her if we can measure it
bring my tape

I'm still alive you know Gladys says
when she sees me wheeling you
down the hallway to her room.

    Sorry to disturb you once again I tell her.

    If you want to see the room again, I tell my father,
    you're on your own.

Rattling Down the Chimney

We sit in your room,
eat chocolates, drink ginger ale,
plug in the lamp and Christmas lights
you bought at the nursing home bazaar.

You have cut the lamp shade
so the lamp fits tight in the corner
on your rosewood table.

You tell me to take the Christmas lights,
the lamp, a clock and a lunch box home.

>   *I have too much stuff in my room*
>   *don't give it away*
>   *I want it all back*
>   *when I get that bigger room*

Two Things

*Your mother got a kidney infection
in the liberation camp we lived in after the war.*

*Her kidney infection started in a camp not far from Dora
where she was installing underground telephone cables
in the cold.*

*I carried her to the hospital.
There were no beds available.
She would have died
but I spoke to a man outside the hospital
who had just been discharged
so I carried her back inside.
She lost a kidney,
luckily they had a dialysis machine so she lived.*

*I survived concentration camp didn't I ?
Your mother lived after losing a kidney
that's a miracle isn't it?*

*I got over diabetes
and my blood sugar is normal most days*

*I'll beat Parkinson's too you'll see;
then I'm going home
I'll ask God to give me another miracle.*

What's the other thing you wanted to tell me?

*Mother was too soft with you
and didn't let me interfere;
you turned out all right.*

Tool Chests

After breakfast you rearrange your binders,
tighten and retighten screws in your lamp,
cut electrical cords with your tools,
clean your room.

When you bend over to wash the floor with a wet rag
you fall out of your wheelchair.

The day nurse uses the lifting machine to get you back in.

>*Your dad's a piece of work* she says

and the night nurse asks me to take my dad's tool chests home.

>*He'll hurt himself,*

but he says

>*I need my tools. It's my room.*
>*I'm a registered safety professional.*
>*Here's my card.*
>
>*Life is like a baby's diaper*
>*short and shitty.*

Disappearing

I'm not too bad for an 82-year-old guy

    You're 89.

show me the math; son of a gun I'm 89

    How do you feel today, Dad?

*how would you feel if you were losing your mind
and knew it*

*I'm going back to the other nursing home
it doesn't make sense to pay for two rooms*

    You mean your condo? Where Emily lives now?

*no there's no room 168 here
look at my bracelet
what does it say*

    Room 168 Elm House

*someone is lying to me don't talk to the nurses
they're in on it too call a lawyer
help me pack I'm moving*

    Do you want me to pack your books
    and binders in these green crates?

*does your brother live with you
he was here a minute ago I'm worried about him
he's not working he needs money*

Dad, you know he's dead.
What does he need money for?

I know he's dead but if he's going to visit me
he needs five dollars for lunch in the dining room
I asked him if he needed money he disappeared

Future Gardens

Deep in their roots, all flowers keep the light.
—Theodore Roethke

The hum of bees was an excuse
to lament the gardens you'd never live to see

turbulent years slipping like a knotted string unravelling
and over dessert your heart bled sweetness
was like honey spreading, leaving a grainy film.

Your words blunt knives
with a silence of uncertainty and imprecision
not stabbing but leaving a mark,
even your whispers awake
and I couldn't rest
but fell in with the rhythms of your dying;
there was no way to change the rules.

Documents missing their plastic sleeves
lie scattered on the floor.

No One Can

A nurse takes your vitals: blood pressure critically low,
blood sugar, high. You're asleep before she's done.

My grandson in his Spider Man costume sings
Spider Man, Spider Man if he can't do it no one can.

Vase of stargazer lilies, red carnations, baby's breath.
I trim dead leaves and flowers with your nail scissors.

No resuscitation. Comfort care only, is that correct?
Yes, that's what my dad wants.

Petals fall one by one, leave a trail of yellow pollen.
A week late one lily remains, then it too is gone.

Exhale

Forty-eight hours to clear your room,
a wedding portrait of you and Mother,
my brother and I as teenagers and

your first great grandson on your lap,
the great granddaughter you never met
born a week before you died

oatmeal raisin cookies, chocolate-covered
plums and ginger ale from the fridge,
your electric shaver.

We pack your favourite vest with seven pockets,
bridge books, tool chests, Polish cassettes,
Silesia porcelain and Seth Thomas clock

leave the flat screen TV and La-Z-Boy chair
carry boxes of binders that hold your life
open the door to let the room exhale.

Auction

One hundred pieces
of gold-rimmed Silesia porcelain:
hand-painted roses and peonies
on serving plates, bowls, pitchers
huddled like orphaned children—
lots 112, 113, 114.

In a dream, my mother hands me
a purple velvet purse filled with silver coins
as I carefully pack your treasures, tells me
it's all right to sell things, or give them away.
You, Dad, nod in the background.

Counter-Clockwise

I open the glass over its face,
align the hour and minute hands
to the precise time,
insert the brass butterfly key,

rotate counter-clockwise
until it stops turning
just as you showed me.

Your Seth Thomas clock tick tocks
in a patterned dance, awakens the past,
all the antique clocks you restored
measure time on walls and mantles.

On our basement shelves
your store of mainsprings,
pendulums and sprockets.

the universe is a clock you said
how can there not be a God

I Never Had the Chance

I never had the chance
to hold you before you died.

Instead I covered your cold legs
with a green woolen throw

massaged lavender-scented foot cream
into your diabetic feet

dampened your face and neck with a warm facecloth,
spread mounds of Foamy on your sensitive skin

shaved you carefully with a straight blade
until I could almost hear you say *that will do*

while you examined every fold of skin
for stray hair and I thought of how

you patted my shoulder and gave me
a brief hug when I was done.

Lately, Everything is Language

A red wing evokes
flushed cheeks.
Translucent air reveals
winter's landscape.

A crow's
unblinking eyes follow me
from tree to tree as I walk.

Branches wave
in a different alphabet.
Your voice murmurs
through the pines.

April is here again
without you.

The memory recalls all,
traces of mint candy,
steaming cups of cocoa.

My heart carries you.
A noun, any noun
an anchor.

Locked in Different Alphabets

Locked in Different Alphabets

My Mother,

Sasanka,

Means

Wild Flower

Locked in Different Alphabets

Ashes

In place of ruins—
a new Warsaw full of life,
beautiful, new, just like before the war.

Where Mother's ashes are buried
red geraniums
flower.

My Parents Remember

Stepping on something soft—a dead child's hand,
war planes spewing fire on their landscape

men and women hanging in the streets,
the stomp of black boots past buildings,
children herded into cattle cars.

After the war running, running, running away,
turning off the sounds in their heads.

Babcia (Grandmother)

In Canada, my babcia chanted Hail Marys on her knees,
to Saint Francis of Assisi she asked *make me an instrument*

of thy peace but faulted her daughter's posture, her ways
of dusting, criticized clothes, hair, and curtain choices.

My father and Babcia didn't speak *to keep the peace* he said,
when they forgot they weren't talking words scorched the air.

She cooked blueberry pierogi for my brother but only offered me
her life of sorrows, parents dead from Spanish flu, death

illness, miscarriage, twin boys that lived a week.
Where there is despair, hope. In her last few weeks

I manicured her nails, applied red polish and warmed her hands.
You must be able to hear how hard my heart is beating she said.

Where there is darkness, light.

I Knew

The events of childhood do not pass but repeat themselves like seasons of the year. —Eleanor Farjeon

Even in this fresh landscape
shadows veiled the sun,
wild flowers burned to ashes

overloaded plates of pierogi,
pickled herring and sauerkraut
covered our table

rows of Maxwell House jars,
tins of Habitant pea soup
crammed our basement shelves

dresses, price tags still attached,
hung like war-starved ghosts
in Mother's closet.

Sasanka (Wild Flower)

At the first thunder clap

my mother locked herself in the bathroom

couldn't speak, refused to come out

until the storm was over.

Before the Warsaw Uprising

I was a Girl Scout in the Polish Home Army.

My pseudonym name was Sasanka.

In front of our house, a German tank was firing.

At sunrise we thought Poland was ours.

She hated cramped dark spaces

was afraid to fly

never answered the door to strangers

endured high risk pregnancies

with long confinements.

My mother and I worked bandaging wounded soldiers.

On the hospital's staircase, we heard a bomb explode.

My mother removed bricks with her hands

looking for my father's body

until a German plane started shooting in our direction

Her doctor treated hand tremors
high blood pressure
recurring bladder infections

Locked in Different Alphabets

                                       at night, people dug graves and
                                       buried their loved ones

chest and back pain
panic attacks
                                  the smell of the dead was overpowering

nightmares
                                        especially during sunny days

                                            heat from burning houses
                                        scorched our bodies and hair

                            I was afraid to let go of my mother's hand
                            while she was looking for my father's body

When my mother forgot her pill
                                                      especially
she awoke—
                                          the smell of the dead

Słoneczko

'I'm fine' I always said
whenever my parents asked.
Father held me tight on the bobsled.

Mother's love, a hefty wool blanket,
that warmed our home.
Still, they couldn't shield me

from their war-time trauma, though
I wasn't starved in Nazi camps
forced to labour from daybreak to dusk,

I knew nothing of hungering for a country
or weeping for those who had perished.
Grief shadowed them

from room to room. *I'm fine.*
Little ray of sunshine—
my mother's endearment for me.

Without Warning

Wind's rough hand pushes
me here and there,
uprooted trees stretch
rain-darkened tentacles,
grab my ankles,
thrash a car's windshield
with roots and dirt.

I'm lost, on a crowded beach
after slipping from my mother's grip
to look for my white socks
left on the shore.

I awaken
chilled.

My Mother Said

Before our home burned down
at 1 Mirowska Street in Warsaw
I sketched a song sparrow
perched on the window sill and collected
clusters of blushing peonies
in the backyard.

Before my childhood snapped shut like a fox cage
I helped my mother cut dough circles
for Christmas Eve pierogi,
filled their centres with sauerkraut and mushrooms
and sealed their edges with my fingers.

Before I ceased being that girl
Luba and I linked arms,
crossed the street to the bakery,
revealed a secret
over plum-filled pastries
and cocoa.

After the bomb blast
I searched for traces of my father
found one leather glove
smoldering.

Bell's Corners

What a God-forsaken place my artist mother said.
She wore two-inch heels on our unpaved street,
insisted on skirts, only resorted to comfortable shoes

to roam the woods behind our house.
We picked wild mushrooms, shared space
with wandering cows.

When the bookmobile came
we were first inside and I asked how many books
we could take home. *As many as you can carry.*

That summer my mother painted red poppies
and purple lilac bouquets; she sketched portraits
of me under our linden tree lost

in the pages of *Lassie*. Now a book of Polish verse
lies on my night table with a wisp of hair
I carefully trimmed

and placed in an envelope when she died
bookmarks *Kaczka-Dziwaczka,* or *The Eccentric Duck*
our favourite.

Labour

In the dream I birthed
seven pairs of white socks

they slipped out easily
each set rolled into a soft ball

velvety as a newborn rabbit
I placed them with care in a wicker basket

beneath a warm wool blanket
seven is a lucky number my mother said

you will have a healthy boy
remember to keep your feet warm

Dreams Over and Over

My mother leaves my brother and me
in front of the mall,
waves, drives off.

By the water behind my childhood cottage
she warns *don't swim out too far,*
walks away, doesn't look.

In hospital she stared at her frozen
arm, leg; her mouth and tongue
twisted familiar words

refused the ice chips.
The night after she died, I dreamt
of her crawling from a tiny wooden box

stuffed with oversized pillows.
She opened her arms to me saying

I was trapped inside.
She is as near as the horned owl
perched in the pine tree

or the fox hiding in its musky haunts.
Some nights she sits in the empty chair beside me,
strokes my cheek and whispers my name.

In Each Other's Dreams

You and I strolled Warsaw's streets
my mother said.

I told her I saw her wave
from the living room window
of our Montreal home on Montgomery Street.

After she died
I wandered as though in a ghostly wood.

Wind—
my only confidante.

We tend
a crow with a broken wing.

It will fly again she says.

Salt Spray

my mother's breath
on the back of my neck,
a light touch on the shoulder,
she and I walk on sand
under a limitless sky.

We breathe salt spray
as she points out the curves
of distant islands.

You can't travel there she says.

I hold her when we say good-bye.

I stay on shore,
watch waves shift shapes, catch
glimpses of her face in the water.

She was always so afraid
of drowning.

Locked in Different Alphabets

Understanding My Mother's Worries

A night of teal and tangerine, my clothes
thrown together in hurried mismatch,
my daughter Natalia's panicked call.

After my daughter's panicked call
about her daughter's seal bark, laboured breath,
her fevered skin

I remember my own mother's worries when I was sick,
her nights of teal and tangerine,
my fevered skin.

I stay with my grandson as he slumbers spread-eagled
on his stomach in bed, I am reading *Far to Go:*
A Jewish mother

repacks her son's suitcase, adds galoshes,
a diamond watch, medicine, a family photo
and sends him away on the Kindertransport.

Natalia returns at dawn, her daughter in her arms,
my grandson sleeps on as if the night were seamless …
as if the night were seamless.

Passenger

On the rare days she had to herself
without my father following her
from room to room
wanting to know what she was doing

my mother painted, studied art techniques,
landscape artists and the paranormal,
savoured a coffee and Du Maurier in the den,
her secret pleasures.

While driving, now and then, it seems
that out of the corner of my eye
I glimpse the glowing tip
and a curl of rising smoke.

Foraging

We hike for hours without luck
but on rare occasions we're rewarded
with an endless hoard
of yellow chanterelles
or elusive morels,
setting each one carefully in our baskets.

At home we devour sautéed boletes
in butter with onions and scrambled eggs
for a late lunch.

My mother and I work fast
to dehydrate the rest while still fresh.
We clean each one gently
with a small soft brush,

separate stem from cap,
placing them on foil-lined racks
in a slow oven,
turning them after an hour,
letting them slowly dry for another.

The scent of drying fungi
lingers in the kitchen for days;
all winter they end up
in her goulash.

Snapshot 3

He strides over to where I stand
hands me his 35-millimetre Minolta.

I don't need it where I am my father laughs.
He straightens his tie,
squeezes into his suit jacket.

A rabbi and a priest he says
are stopped by Saint Peter at the Pearly Gates…
he stumbles on the punchline.

Father, Mother and Babcia float at the base
of a mountain beneath a kaleidoscope sky.

My mother blows me a coral-coloured kiss,
checks lipstick in a compact mirror.
George cycles out of an elephant-shaped cloud
wearing bike shorts and a purple tie-dyed T-shirt.
Babcia fingers her black rosary.

Use the right exposure my father says.

Let her do it her way my mother says.

Babcia smiles, cuddles into George, cradles his arm.

Take the picture George says. *I don't have all day.*

Zen Garden

Nature does not hurry, and yet everything is accomplished.
—Taoist proverb

Comb smooth stones into still spaces,
rake ripples into a curving river, follow its seasons

through spring splurges of daffodils and azaleas,
jack-in-the-pulpits and pink lady slippers,

sweetened islands of midsummer roses clustering
honey bees in their orange heads.

Remember when water lilies—rose-coloured teacups
on emerald saucers—bobbed up and down in the pond.

Then in winter, deer wobbled over icy mounds,
nibbling loose corn in the bare-bones yard.

Now purple New England asters, native grasses and nasturtiums
linger into chill. Sit on the stone bench.
A rake rests against the maple.

Let your breath become unhurried,
as the trees that surround the garden.

Nod inwardly at each thought
as if it were a withering leaf.

Breathe in morning silence.
Exhale morning silence.

    A sugar-swollen monarch
        will shiver its way to warmth.

Notes and Acknowledgements

Many thanks to the editors of both my chapbooks: '*The Binder's*, Tree Press, 2016 and '*Sasanka (Wild Flower')*, Bywords Publishing, 2018 where a number of these poems have previously appeared, often in different versions.

I am grateful to the following journals and anthologies where some of these poems have also appeared, or will soon appear: *ottawater, PoetrySuperHighway.com*, '*Bywords Quarterly Journal*', *bywords.ca, Juniper: 'A Poetry Journal', 'Motherhood in Precarious Times'*, Demeter Press 2018, '*Tamaracks Canadian Poetry for the 21st Centur'y*, Lummox Press 2018.

I am grateful to poetry judge Gillian Sze who selected "Zen Garden" for the 2017 John Newlove Poetry Award.

Many thanks to Ruby Tuesdays for their friendship, continuing support and careful reading of my poems. Their insightful comments have enhanced my writing.

I am also thankful for having had the opportunity to be a member of other poetry groups: a poetry group that meets monthly, initially under the leadership of Deanna Young, then Nadine McInnis, and subsequently David O'Meara and earlier groups under the guidance of Stephanie Bolster and the late Barbara Myers.

My gratitude to Claudia Coutu Radmore for her ongoing and invaluable guidance allowing me to first envision my poetry in a chapbook format, '*The Binders'*, and finally as a larger manuscript spanning my family's life.

I offer thanks to Candice James, publisher and editor of Silver Bow Publishing who turned my dream of publishing my manuscript into a reality. Thank you!

I am also grateful to the people who have read and offered their input on my manuscript in its earlier versions. Warm thanks to Deanna Young and Mark Frutkin for their insightful critiques of my poetry.

Immense love and gratitude to my loyal friends who never tired of hearing my poems as they evolved and have applauded all my successes.

Deep appreciation and love to my family who have supported my writing practice. Thanks to my sons Joshua and Christopher for enthusiastically attending all my poetry events.

Finally, a special thank you to my husband Bruce whose careful reading, positive comments and discussion of all my poems were instrumental in motivating me to complete my manuscript.

In "Dreams Over and Over" the line *"walks away, doesn't look"* was adapted from "Two Dreams" in '*Morning in the Burned House*' by Margaret Atwood.

www.ingramcontent.com/pod-product-compliance
Lightning Source LLC
Chambersburg PA
CBHW070940080526
44589CB00013B/1581